1996 E

Suggested Solutions

Public International Law

LLB

University of London
External Examinations

Solutions by Jonathan Miller
LLB, Dip Int Rel, LLM

HLT Publications

HLT PUBLICATIONS
200 Greyhound Road, London W14 9RY

Reprinted 1998

ISBN 0 7510 0762 5

British Library Cataloguing-in-Publication.

A CIP Catalogue record for this book is available from the British Library.

Printed and bound in Great Britain.

CONTENTS

ACKNOWLEDGEMENT

The questions used are taken from the University of London LLB (External) Degree examination paper and our thanks are extended to the University of London for the kind permission which has been given to us to use and publish the questions.

Caveat

The answers given are not approved or sanctioned by the University of London and are entirely our responsibility.

They are not intended as 'Model Answers', but rather as Suggested Solutions.

The answers have two fundamental purposes, namely:

a) To provide a detailed example of a suggested solution to examination questions, and

b) To assist students with their research into the subject and to further their understanding and appreciation of the subject.

Note

Please note that the solutions in this book were written in the year of the examination. They were appropriate solutions at the time of preparation, but students must note that certain caselaw and statutes may subsequently have changed.

INTRODUCTION

Why choose HLT publications?

Holborn College has earned an international reputation for the outstanding quality of its teaching, Textbooks, Casebooks and Suggested Solutions to past examination papers.

Our expertise is reflected in the outstanding results achieved by our students in the examinations conducted by the University of London LLB Honours Degree Programme for External Students, the Council of Legal Education, and by students in over 70 universities who use our publications.

Suggested Solutions

The Suggested Solutions series provides examples of full answers to the problems posed by examiners. The solutions are much more than answers achievable by a candidate under examination conditions. The opportunity has been taken, where appropriate, to develop themes, suggest alternatives and set out additional material providing further comprehensive topical coverage.

To aid comprehension and revision, the solutions are fuller than would be possible under examination conditions. It is important to keep in mind that at this level there almost certainly is more than just one approach in answering any given question.

We feel that in writing full opinion answers we can assist you with your research and further your understanding and appreciation of the law.

Notes on examination technique

Although the SUBSTANCE and SLANT of the answer changes according to the subject-matter of the question, the examining body and syllabus concerned, the TECHNIQUE of answering examination questions does not change.

You will not pass an examination if you do not know the substance of a course. You may pass if you do not know how to go about answering a question although this is doubtful. To do well and to guarantee success, however, it is necessary to learn the technique of answering problems properly. The following is a guide to acquiring that technique.

Time

All examinations permit only a limited time for papers to be completed. All papers require you to answer a certain number of questions in that time, and the questions, with some exceptions carry equal marks.

It follows from this that you should never spend a disproportionate amount of time on any question. When you have used up the amount of time allowed for any one question STOP and go on to the next question after an abrupt conclusion, if necessary. If you feel that you are running out of time, then complete your answer in note form. A useful way of ensuring that you do not over-run is to write down on a piece of scrap paper the time at which you should be starting each part of the paper. This can be done in the few minutes before the examination begins and it will help you to calm any nerves you may have.

Reading the question

It will not be often that you will be able to answer every question on an examination paper. Inevitably, there will be some areas in which you feel better prepared than others. You will prefer to answer the questions which deal with those areas, but you will never know how good the questions are unless you read the whole examination paper.

You should spend at least 10 MINUTES at the beginning of the examination reading the questions. Preferably, you should read them more than once. As you go through each question, make a brief note on the examination paper of any relevant cases and/or statutes that occur to you even if you think you may not answer that question: you may well be grateful for this note towards the end of the examination when you are tired and your memory begins to fail.

Re-reading the answers

Ideally, you should allow time to re-read your answers. This is rarely a pleasant process, but will ensure that you do not make any silly mistakes such as leaving out a 'not' when the negative is vital.

The structure of the answer

Almost all examination problems raise more than one legal issue that you are required to deal with. Your answer should:

Identify the issues raised by the question
This is of crucial importance and gives shape to the whole answer. It indicates to the examiner that you appreciate what he is asking you about.

This is at least as important as actually answering the questions of law raised by that issue.

The issues should be identified in the first paragraph of the answer.

Deal with those issues one by one as they arise in the course of the problem
This, of course, is the substance of the answer and where study and revision pays off.

If the answer to an issue turns on a provision of a statute, CITE that provision briefly, but do not quote it from any statute you may be permitted to bring into the examination hall
Having cited the provision, show how it is relevant to the question.

If there is no statute, or the meaning of the statute has been interpreted by the courts, CITE the relevant cases
'Citing cases' does not mean writing down the name of every case that happens to deal with the general topic with which you are concerned and then detailing all the facts you can think of.

You should cite only the most relevant cases – there may perhaps only be one. No more facts should be stated than are absolutely essential to establish the relevance of the case. If there is a relevant case, but you cannot remember its name, it is sufficient to refer to it as 'one decided case'.

Whenever a statute or case is cited, the title of statute or the name of the case should be underlined
This makes the examiner's job much easier because he can see at a glance whether the relevant material has been dealt with, and it will make him more disposed in your favour.

Having dealt with the relevant issues, summarise your conclusions in such a way that you answer the question
A question will often say at the end simply 'Advise A', or B, or C, etc. The advice will usually turn on the individual answers to a number of issues. The point made here is that the final paragraph should pull those individual answers together and actually give the advice required. For example, it may begin something like: 'The effect of the answer to the issues raised by this question is that one's advice to A is that ...'

Related to the previous paragraph, make sure at the end that you have answered the question
For example, if the question says 'Advise A', make sure that is what your answer does. If you are required to advise more than one party, make sure that you have dealt with all the parties that you are required to and no more.

Some general points

You should always try to get the examiner on your side. One method has already been mentioned – the underlining of case names, etc. There are also other ways as well.

Always write as neatly as you can. This is more easily done with ink than with a ball-point.

Avoid the use of violently coloured ink eg turquoise; this makes a paper difficult to read.

Space out your answers sensibly: leave a line between paragraphs. You can always get more paper. At the same time, try not to use so much paper that your answer book looks too formidable to mark. This is a question of personal judgment.

NEVER put in irrelevant material simply to show that you are clever. Irrelevance is not a virtue and time spent on it is time lost for other, relevant, answers.

EXAMINATION PAPER

UNIVERSITY OF LONDON
LLB EXAMINATIONS 1996
for External Students
PART II EXAMINATION (Scheme A)
THIRD AND FOURTH YEAR EXAMINATIONS (Scheme B)
GRADUATE ENTRY LEVEL II (Route A)
GRADUATE ENTRY THIRD YEAR (Route B)

PUBLIC INTERNATIONAL LAW

Tuesday, 4 June: 10.00 am to 1.00 pm

Answer *FOUR* of the following NINE questions

1 Assess the importance of opinio juris in the creation of rules of international law.

2 What problems does a municipal court face in dealing with the legal capacity, constitution and powers of an international organisation?

3 States K and L have made unconditional declarations accepting the jurisdiction of the International Court of Justice (ICJ) under art 36(2) of the Statute of the Court. State M has made a declaration accepting the jurisdiction of the ICJ but excluding 'matters falling within the scope of the criminal jurisdiction of State M'. Fernandez, a national of State M, currently residing in State L, conspired with six nationals of K to overthrow the government of State K. Before the plan is executed, however, the seven are arrested by the police of State L and charged with criminal conspiracy, to be tried in the courts of State L. The government of State K seeks to have all seven of the accused extradited to State K where mandatory death sentences are imposed on conviction for criminal conspiracy against the government. The government of State M fears that Fernandez will receive harsh treatment in the courts of State L and seeks to have him extradited for trial in State M. Recently, the courts of State L refused extradition applications from both States K and M, on the grounds that only State L had jurisdiction in respect of

the alleged offences. Both States K and M claim concurrent jurisdiction and are separately considering reference of the issue to the ICJ.

Advise States K and M on:

a) the jurisdiction of the ICJ over their representative claims; and

b) the merits of their claims to jurisdiction over Fernandez.

4 a) 'The Vienna Convention on Diplomatic Relations, 1961, requires radical revision.'

Discuss.

b) State A's authorities suspect that Edvard, a member of the staff of State B's diplomatic mission to State A, is engaged in drug smuggling activities. Assuming that both States are parties to the Vienna Convention on Diplomatic Relations, 1961, advise State A's authorities as to whether they may:

i) subject the diplomatic bag of State B to electronic surveillance;

ii) search the private residence of Edvard and of his driver, Maria, who is a national of State A;

iii) arrest Edvard and Maria when they attend a meeting with suspected drug dealers outside the capital of State A; and

iv) expel the ambassador of State B for failing to prevent the alleged drug smuggling activities.

5 The population of the State of Despairia consists of two ethnic groups, the Wabenzi, who make up 60 per cent of the population and who control the government and the armed forces, and the Ba-Audi, who comprise the remaining 40 per cent. After an outbreak of unrest amongst the Ba-Audi minority, many Ba-Audi have been arrested and their villages burned by government troops. The situation has provoked a mass exodus of Ba-Audi refugees into the neighbouring State of Zenubia, causing there major economic problems and a breakdown of law and order.

Zenubia has approached the Security Council of the United Nations, asking for authority to intervene in Despairia in order to enforce the establishment of a protected zone for the Ba-Audi people. The government of Despairia has warned that any intervention within its territory would amount to a flagrant breach of fundamental principles of international law as incorporated in the United Nations Charter.

Advise Zenubia as to:

a) how the Security Council is likely to respond to Zenubia's request; and

b) whether, in the event of no action being taken by the Security Council, international law entitles Zenubia to intervene unilaterally?

6 To what extent do individuals possess procedural capacity in global and regional regimes established for the protection of human rights?

7 a) Why was the incorporation of the concept of jus cojens into the Vienna Convention on the Law of Treaties, 1961, a source of controversy?

b) In 1996, Arcadia, a former colony of Imperia, obtained independence after a long struggle for national liberation. The new foreign minister of Arcadia seeks your advice on the following matters:

i) Arcadia's obligations, if any, in respect of a treaty concluded in 1982 by Imperia under which a substantial part of the then colony of Arcadia was transferred to the neighbouring State of Sindaria in return for military assistance against the Arcadian Liberation Front;

ii) Arcadia's wish to become a party to a United Nations Convention on Compulsory Dispute Settlement subject to a reservation excluding disputes with Imperia in respect of any matters arising before Arcadia's independence.

8 GTZ is a public limited company incorporated in State S which owns 51 per cent of Cidecorp, an arms manufacturing company incorporated under the laws of State T. Recently, Cidecorp sold an anti-aircraft missile system to the Beta Liberation Movement (BLM), an organisation which seeks independence for the people residing in the Beta region of State U. When the BTM ordered the missile system, it made no secret of its intention to use the missiles against State U's military aircraft. Three days after the missile system was installed, it was used to shoot down a reconnaissance aircraft belonging to the State U airforce, resulting in the deaths of six members of the crew and of four military advisers from State V.

Prepare a memorandum considering any claims that might arise in international law in respect of the deaths.

Ch 11 ✓ 9 'The 1994 Agreement relating to the "implementation" of the United Nations Convention on the Law of the Sea, 1982, represents a victory for states opposed to the principles originally embodied in Part XI of the Convention.'

Discuss.

SUGGESTED SOLUTIONS

QUESTION 1

Assess the importance of opinio juris in the creation of rules of international law.

SUGGESTED SOLUTION TO QUESTION 1

General Comment

This is a rather narrow question. The candidate should be able to define what is meant by opinio juris and analyse how it works in practice. Two of the leading cases (see below) need to be examined as well as the attitude of the ICJ towards the Universal Declaration on Human Rights and GA Resolution 1514. The position of the post-1945 states needs to be considered as well as the wording of art 53 Law of Treaties 1969.

Skeleton Solution

Introduction – the practice of states.

Psychological aspect and definition of opinio juris.

North Sea Continental Shelf Cases.

Lotus Case.

Universal Declaration on Human Rights and GA Res 1514.

Position of 'new states'.

Common consent of states.

Regional customary law and opinio juris.

Conclusion.

Suggested Solution

Customary law is in part to be found in the practice of States in relation to each other. In the Hellenistic international system, for example, the rules which applied to diplomatic immunity and the regulations governing the declaration of war and the signing of peace treaties arose from practices of the Greek city states. Once such a usage has taken on the form of, inter alia, predictability, certainty and uniformity it has gone part of the way into metamorphosing into a rule of customary international law. It is not enough on its own to classify a particular usage, however certain in its definition, as a customary rule.

What is missing to complete the picture is the psychological aspect of the behaviour of States. The opinio juris direction of international law assumes that the usage is regarded by States as having an obligatory character. This may be compared to the traditional theory of conventions in British constitutional law. It is by the obligatory character of the States' practices that a customary rule will be formed, as opposed to a State practice which States will follow because they are minded so to do rather than being obliged as a matter of law. This distinction was discussed in the *North Sea Continental Shelf Cases* (1), where the ICJ held:

> 'Not only must the acts concerned amount to a settled practice, but they must also be such, or be carried out in such a way, as to be evidence of a belief that this practice is rendered obligatory by the existence of a rule of law requiring it ... the States concerned must therefore feel that they are conforming to what amounts to a legal obligation. The frequency, or even habitual character of the acts is not in itself enough.'

Whether a State wishes to avail itself of a customary rule of law is that State's privilege. The fact that the rule is only used in an intermittent manner does not invalidate its character. This was considered in the *Lotus Case: France* v *Turkey* (2). A collision took place on the High Seas between a French ship, the *Lotus*, and a Turkish ship, the *Boz-Kourt*. A number of individuals on board the Turkish ship were drowned and Turkey alleged that the French officer of the watch had been negligent in his duties. When the *Lotus* entered Istanbul harbour and Turkish territorial waters the French officer of the watch was arrested and charged with manslaughter.

The issue for the Permanent Court was to ascertain whether Turkey had jurisdiction to try the French officer. In order to establish or refute this contention the Court had to determine whether there was a rule of law denying or supporting this jurisdiction. The Turkish argument was based on the premise of a permissive rule of international law. This meant that Turkey was permitted to try the individual but not compelled so to do. France argued the contrary, saying that Turkey was under an obligation not to try the officer.

The Court supported the argument of Turkey. It held that although there were only a limited number of cases in which States had acted in the way that Turkey had, nevertheless the other States involved in those cases had not protested. The question to be asked, the Court argued, was not whether States had refrained from prosecution, but whether they felt obliged to refrain. The answer is that they abstained from initiating judicial proceedings of their own free will.

The conclusion from the above is that a new rule of customary law may be formed by States carrying out certain actions and other States failing to protest. Thus it would appear that an objection, and indeed a single State's protest, could prevent a new practice of States taking on an obligatory character. Customary international law has therefore to receive either active or passive approval.

This may be illustrated by examining the nature of General Assembly Resolutions. General Assembly Resolutions have no constitutional authority to create norms of international law. The majority of GA Resolutions are not therefore legally binding. Some Resolutions may, however, reflect the opinio juris of States on a limited number of issues. How, then, is this determined? The voting pattern is crucial. If there are any votes against a GA Resolution then that Resolution is incapable of forming customary international law. If on the contrary there are no votes against and only a limited number of abstentions then the Resolution may evolve into a rule of customary international law. For instance, the Universal Declaration of Human Rights 1948 was initially supported as just that, a declaration. It did not attract any votes against it, and was passed by a vote of 48 to 0 with eight abstentions. This and its subsequent adoption in international documents and general approval might have changed its character.

In the *Namibia (South West Africa) Case* (3) Vice President Ammoun stated:

> 'Although the affirmations of the Declaration are not binding qua international convention ... they can bind States on the basis of custom ... whether because they are constituted a codification of customary law or because they have acquired the force of custom through a general practice accepted as law.'

Similarly with the Declaration on the Granting of Independence to Colonial Peoples (Res 1514), the self-determination Resolution. The pattern of voting might indicate its transformation into a binding obligation: there were no votes against and nine abstentions.

All the above assumes that all States are present to object to a creation of a rule of customary international law, which is obviously not the case. The majority of States have come into existence following the collapse of the Western European empires and latterly with the collapse of the Soviet Union. These States are bound by already existing customary international law even though they were not in existence to object to any aspect of it.

Thus far it has been assumed that the acceptance of any obligation has to be unanimous. Not all the authorities agree on this, thereby opening the way for a more fertile development of customary law. As it has been seen, an abstention in the General Assembly does not signify as an objection. Moreover in *West Rand Central Gold Mining Co* v *R* (4) the English court was prepared to talk about the 'common consent of civilised nations' as forming law which the municipal tribunals (of the United Kingdom) would apply. What amounts to a 'common consent' was not elaborated upon. This line of reasoning is also found in art 53 of the Vienna Convention 1969 on the Law of Treaties, which states that a norm of jus cogens must be 'accepted and recognised by the international community of States *as a whole*' (5).

International customary law may also exist on a regional level and the same requirement of obligation is needed. If an obligation is asserted in respect of a local practice the State making the assertion is required to show that the practice flows from a legal requirement rather than a regional usage. Such was the situation in relation to Portugal's right of passage over Indian territory from its colony in Goa. This 'right of passage' was recognised by both Portugal and India as being obligatory: *Right of Passage over Indian Territory Case: Portugal* v *India* (6).

In order for a practice or usage to become customary international law the States of the world community must regard themselves as being bound by the custom. An objection to a practice will prevent it becoming part of customary international law. Acceptance may be active or passive (not objecting), but there must be this acceptance. Whether the acceptance has to be unanimous or by general consent is open to question.

References

(1) (1969) ICJ Rep p3
(2) (1927) PCIJ Rep Series A No 10
(3) *Legal Consequences for States of the Continued Presence of South Africa in Namibia (South West Africa) Case* (1971) ICJ Rep p16 at p55
(4) [1905] 2 KB 391
(5) See the Suggested Solution to Question 7(a) for an elaboration of this doctrine
(6) (1960) ICJ Rep p6

QUESTION 2

What problems does a municipal court face in dealing with the legal capacity, constitution and powers of an international organisation?

SUGGESTED SOLUTION TO QUESTION 2

General Comment

In order to answer this question in a satisfactory manner it is, the writer submits, necessary to consider how the courts of a particular jurisdiction deal with the problem. Analysis of the approach of the United Kingdom courts to this issue is required, with detailed examination of the relevant case law. The candidate will need an understanding of the *Tin Council Case, Arab Monetary Fund* v *Hashim* and *Westland Helicopters Ltd* v *Arab Organisation for Industrialisation*. The relationship between international law and municipal law needs to be understood.

Skeleton Solution

Introduction – status of international organisations.

Monism and dualism.

J H Rayner v *Department of Trade and Industry* (*Tin Council Case*).

International Organisations Act 1968.

AMF v *Hashim*.

Westland Helicopters v *AOI*.

Trendtex Trading Corp v *Central Bank of Nigeria*.

Conclusion.

Suggested Solution

Whether or not an international organisation is a legal personality and therefore a subject of international law may be ascertained from the treaty setting it up or its personality may be ascertained by examining its functions. The leading authority on this matter is contained in an Advisory Opinion of the ICJ in the *Reparations for Injuries Suffered in the Service of the UN* (1). The Court was of the opinion that the UN had an international legal personality so that it could achieve its international functions as laid out in the Charter.

The Court opined that:

'... fifty States, representing the vast majority of the members of the international community, had the power, in conformity with international law, to bring into being an entity possessing objective international personality, and not merely personality recognised by them alone ...'

While the above provides a guideline for the international community it does not, however, provide a definitive answer for the municipal courts as to whether an international organisation has a legal capacity in the domestic setting. In order to find a starting point for this discussion it is necessary to consider whether the State concerned adheres to the monistic or dualistic view of international law. According to monism, international law and State law are concomitant aspects of the one system, that is law in general. Dualism, on the other hand, sees international law and municipal law as being separate systems of law operating in their own spheres. If a State adheres to the monistic system then international organisations will present the municipal courts with no problem as to their legal capacity. The courts can ascertain this from looking at the decisions of international tribunals and treaties. If, on the other hand, the municipal law adheres to the dualistic system, then the State's courts may not without domestic intervention utilise international legal decisions or treaties to ascertain the existence of a putative international personality.

This problem was highlighted in the United Kingdom when considering the existence or otherwise of three separate international organisations. In *J H Rayner (Mincing Lane)* v *Department of Trade and Industry* (known as the *Tin Council Case)* (2) the House of Lords was presented with the problem of the status of the International Tin Council. This international organisation was set up by treaty and the United Kingdom courts had to ascertain whether it had a status in English law. In the matter of treaties the United Kingdom courts adhere to the 'transformation approach' whereby treaties do not form part of the law of the United Kingdom unless they are 'transformed' into United Kingdom law by an Act of Parliament. Treaties are signed and ratified by the Crown under its prerogative power so to do and the Crown cannot make laws, only an Act of Parliament can: *Case of Proclamations* (3). A treaty and its terms are not part of the law of the United Kingdom and treaties to which the United Kingdom is a party are not self-executing: they do not create rights and obligations.

Therefore, the United Kingdom Parliament had to pass the International Organisations Act 1968 by which Her Majesty's government by Order in Council had the power to 'confer on [an] organisation the legal capacities of a body corporate' if it is an organisation of which the United Kingdom government is a member or if it maintains or proposes to maintain an establishment in the United Kingdom.

Thus the *Tin Council Case* had to establish whether there was such an Order in Council which invested the Tin Council with a separate legal personality. The House of Lords answered in the affirmative. This did not mean, however, that the Council would be treated in the same manner as a United Kingdom organisation. It was a separate persona ficta created by the Order in Council. Without the Order in Council such an organisation is not a legal person and therefore has no legal capacity. With the Order in Council – which Lord Donaldson MR in *Arab Monetary Fund* v *Hashim* (*No* 3) (4) described as a 'magic wand' – it becomes a person. Lord Donaldson went on to describe it as a person sui generis:

> 'which has all the capacities of a United Kingdom juridical person, but is not subject to the controls to which such a person is subject under United Kingdom law. It is not a native, but nor is it a visitor from abroad. It comes from the invisible depths of outer space.'

The above meant that although the Tin Council was a legal person this did not entail liability for the State-members of the organisation. Lord Oliver in the *Tin Council Case* said:

> 'the ITC though not formally incorporated, was invested with a legal personality distinct from its members, with the consequence that, when it entered into engagements it and not the membership was the contracting party.'

Further problems were raised before the United Kingdom courts when considering the legal status of the Arab Monetary Fund (AMF) (4). In 1976 the Fund was established by international agreement among 20 Arab states and the Palestine Liberation Organisation. Article 2 of the agreement provided that the organisation was to have 'independent judicial personality and ... in particular the right to own, contract and litigate'. The headquarters of the organisation were established in Abu Dhabi. In 1977 the United Arab Emirates passed legislation giving the treaty force of law and thereby conferring legal personality on the AMF, the plaintiff.

Hashim, a former director general of the organisation, was alleged by the plaintiffs to have absconded with around $50 million in funds belonging to the Fund. The plaintiff subsequently found Hashim resident in London and began an action to recover the missing money. In *Arab Monetary Fund* v *Hashim (No 3)* (4) the House of Lords had to consider the legal status of the Fund and whether it was entitled to bring an acton. The United Kingdom had not been a party to the treaty establishing the Fund, nor had the treaty been transformed into English law. Following the reasoning of earlier cases, and in particular the *Tin Council Case*, it would appear that the Fund would have no legal capacity to sue in the United Kingdom courts. However the present case was distinguished in that the Fund was incorporated under the laws of the United Arab Emirates, a State recognised by the United Kingdom, and the United Kingdom courts would recognise a corporate body created by the law of a foreign State so recognised. The AMF was not brought into existence by a treaty in the eyes of the United Kingdom courts, but rather by a decree of a recognised government. This issue is further discussed in *Westland Helicopters Ltd* v *Arab Organisation for Industrialisation* (5). The Divisional Court was again confronted with the issue of an unenacted treaty (ie, not transformed) which had created an international organisation (see below). Coleman J utilised the reasoning in *Arab Monetary Fund* v *Hashim (No 3)* (4), holding that the AOI had legal personality in United Kingdom law as a result of it being incorporated by the law of a recognised State: Egypt.

How then are the English courts to interpret the constitutions and powers of an international organisation which the courts have established exist? An answer to this problem was in part supplied by *Westland Helicopters Ltd* v *Arab Organisation for Industrialisation* (5). Four Arab states (Egypt, United Arab Emirates, Qatar and Saudi Arabia) established by treaty the Arab Organisation for Industrialisation (AOI). The treaty stated that the organisation was to have international personality and that it was not to be governed by the domestic law of any one State. Following a disagreement all the participating States, with the exception of Egypt, called for the Organisation to be disbanded. Egypt, on the other hand, passed a law which purported to take control of the Organisation. The Egyptian law stated that the Organisation was to become an Egyptian legal personality governed by Egyptian law.

Westland Helicopters, following this event, terminated its relationship with the AOI and sued for compensation from the liquidation tribunal of the AOI in Saudi Arabia. Westland failed in this attempt, but after a successful arbitration proceeding in Geneva they sought a garnishee order against British banks which held the AOI funds.

Coleman J in the Divisional Court had to tackle the problem of which law to apply; the Egyptian municipal law or public international law. Egypt claimed that the Egyptian AOI was the successor organisation and that it was therefore the owner of the funds held in the United Kingdom.

Coleman J held that any dispute as to the meaning of the treaty was to be determined by reference to the treaty and to the principles of international law rather than a particular municipal law. If one State's laws were to have priority in the interpretation of the workings of an international organisation this would affront all the other Member States whose laws were to be ignored. It was irrelevant that the Organisation's Headquarters were in Cairo. Inter-State issues are not amenable to resolution by the application of the domestic law of a particular State.

In looking at the constitution and powers of an international organisation the English courts will apply public international law and 'give effect to clearly established rules of international law': *Oppenheimer* v *Cattermole* (6) quoted in *Westland Helicopters* v *AOI* (5). Customary international public law rules will be 'incorporated' into English law by the courts, provided that they are not at variance with the common law or an Act of Parliament. The common law is, however, presumed to be consistent with the principles of international law and the courts will not apply a precedent which is at variance with a new development of international law: *Trendtex Trading Corp* v *Central Bank of Nigeria* (7). Shaw LJ stated in *Trendtex* that 'the English courts must at any given time discover what the prevailing international rule is and apply that rule.'

When dealing with an international organisation, an English court must determine its existence in the eyes of the United Kingdom and then apply the relevant public international law. If an organisation and its parent treaty have not been transformed into domestic law then the court may adopt a creative approach, as demonstrated with the *AMF* (4) and *Westland Helicopters* (5) cases. Having established its existence and capacity, the English court must, in the words of Shaw LJ, 'discover' the international rule before interpreting the constitution and powers of the international organisation.

References

(1) (1949) ICJ Rep p174
(2) [1990] 2 AC 418
(3) (1611) 12 Co Rep 74
(4) [1991] 2 AC 114
(5) [1995] 2 WLR 126
(6) [1976] AC 249
(7) [1977] QB 529

QUESTION 3

States K and L have made unconditional declarations accepting the jurisdiction of the International Court of Justice (ICJ) under art 36(2) of the Statute of the Court. State M has made a declaration accepting the jurisdiction of the ICJ but excluding 'matters falling within the scope of the criminal jurisdiction of State M'. Fernandez, a national of State M, currently residing in State L, conspired with six nationals of K to overthrow the government of State K. Before the plan is executed, however, the seven are arrested by the police of State L and charged with criminal conspiracy, to be tried in the courts of State L. The government of State K seeks to have all seven of the accused extradited to State K where mandatory death sentences are imposed on conviction for criminal conspiracy against the government. The government of State M fears that Fernandez will receive harsh treatment in the courts of State L and seeks to have him extradited for trial in State M. Recently, the courts of State L refused extradition applications from both States K and M, on the grounds that only State L had jurisdiction in respect of the alleged offences. Both States K and M claim concurrent jurisdiction and are separately considering reference of the issue to the ICJ.

Advise States K and M on:

a) the jurisdiction of the ICJ over their representative claims; and

b) the merits of their claims to jurisdiction over Fernandez.

SUGGESTED SOLUTION TO QUESTION 3

General Comment

Part (a) of this question involves a consideration of the jurisdiction of the ICJ. Candidates should be able to discuss the issue of any Preliminary Objections which may be raised to State K's application. With regard to State M, an understanding of the workings of an automatic reservation and the principle of reciprocity is necessary. A discussion of the circumstances under which an extradition may proceed is also required.

Part (b) invites an analysis of the various ways in which a State may claim jurisdiction over an individual. The merits of the claims of States K and M raise different issues and should be dealt with separately. As the question contains a number of different hypotheses no one conclusion is necessary or possible.

Skeleton Solution

a) Jurisdiction of ICJ over the claim of State K.
   South West Africa Cases.
   Political issue.
   State K and extradition.
   State M and automatic reservation.
   State M and reciprocity.

b) State K and protective principle.
   State K and effects doctrine.
   State K and passive personality principle.
   State M and nationality of Fernandez: *Nottebohm.*
   Concurrent jurisdiction and enforcement.

Suggested Solution

a) The jurisdiction of the ICJ over the claim of State K will depend upon whether the claim is of an international character admissible before the Court. As both States K and L have made unconditional declarations accepting the jurisdiction of the Court, State L is likely to submit that although the claim is covered by the principle of reciprocity (see the discussion below) State K's claim is still inadmissible because State K has failed to establish any legal right or interest on its part. Before the ICJ can consider the merits of a particular case it has to consider preliminary objections to its jurisdiction. These objections are usually dealt with in a separate preliminary judgment. State L is likely to submit that the case of State K is not admissible because although it is of an international character State K has not suffered. The plan was not executed before the seven were arrested and State K has no legal right or interest in the enforcement of State L's laws. State L is likely to rely upon the *South West Africa Cases: Ethiopia* v *South Africa; Liberia* v *South Africa* (1). Ethiopia and Liberia, two former members of the League of Nations, in 1960 instituted proceedings against South Africa before the ICJ claiming that South Africa had failed to carry out the obligations imposed upon it by the Mandate, by which it had agreed with the League of Nations to administer the territory. The Court held that South Africa's obligations under the Mandate were owed to the League and not to the individual members of the League. Ethiopia and Liberia had therefore failed to establish any legal right or interest in the matter.

State K will of course seek to distinguish itself from this case as the government of State K was a potential target of the criminal conspiracy. The citizens of State K were also presumably potential targets, as opposed to the position of Ethiopia and Liberia whose citizens were not affected by South Africa's actions in South West Africa.

State L may also argue that the matter is not within the competence of the Court because the issue is a political one rather than a legal one. In such cases some of the members of the Court have argued (for example in the *Nuclear Test Cases: Australia* v *France; New Zealand* v *France* (2)) that the political nature of the dispute will render a matter non-justiciable. This is unlikely to succeed, however, as State L wishes to try the accused for a criminal offence, rather than a political one.

State K would, in any event, having difficulty in establishing that the ICJ should be looking at the matter as there is no duty under customary international law to extradite. A duty to extradite would arise from a treaty and there is no evidence of such a treaty between State L and State K. Moreover, while State L sees the conspiracy as a simple criminal conspiracy, this is not the case with State K, which places a criminal conspiracy against the government in a separate category with a mandatory death sentence, raising the issue that it is a political offence. There is no general duty to extradite for an offence of a political character and State L will argue this.

The position of State M is somewhat different. State M has made a declaration excluding 'matters falling within the scope of the criminal jurisdiction of State M'. This is known as an automatic reservation as it leaves the scope of what is a matter of criminal jurisdiction to State M. The validity and application of such reservations was considered by the ICJ in the *Norwegian Loans Case: France* v *Norway* (3). France brought a claim against Norway under the 'optional clause' on behalf of French holders of Norwegian bonds. The French Declaration which accepted the compulsory jurisdiction of the Court stated:

> 'This Declaration does not apply to differences relating to matters which are essentially within the national jurisdiction as understood by the Government of the French Republic.'

Norway relied upon the French reservation on the principle of reciprocity. A State accepting the jurisdiction of the Court under the optional clause does so, according to art 36(2), only 'in relation to any other State accepting the same obligation'.

The Court accepted Norway's argument and so Norway was able to invoke the reservation contained in the French Declaration.

In this case State L could rely upon State M's reservation, and while it might be problematical that the conspiracy to overthrow the government of State M is a crime under State L's laws, this is a matter for State L. State L may decide what falls within its criminal jurisdiction as State M has reserved that right so to do.

This, of course, undermines the function of the ICJ to determine its jurisdiction. Judge Lauterpacht argued in the *Norwegian Loans Case* (3) that:

> 'the French reservation is ... contrary to one of the most fundamental principles of international – and national – jurisprudence according to which it is within the inherent power of a Tribunal to interpret the text establishing its jurisdiction'.

The party making the reservation is entitled to determine the extent and the very existence of its obligation and therefore State L, relying upon the principle of reciprocity, could argue that the trial of the conspiracy is within its criminal jurisdiction and outside that of the ICJ. State M is unlikely to succeed.

b) State K could claim jurisdiction over Fernandez on the basis of the protective principle. This allows a State to punish acts prejudicial to its security even when they are committed outside the jurisdiction by aliens. In this case Fernandez, a national of State M and therefore an alien in the eyes of State K, entered in to a conspiracy to overthrow the government of State K, clearly a prejudicial act.

State K may also claim jurisdiction on the effects doctrine, ie the effects of the act are harmful to the State. In *R* v *Sansom* (4) jurisdiction was argued on the basis that the effects of the conspiracy, hatched outside the jurisdiction, would be harmful to the United Kingdom, and similarly with the case of *Liangsiriprasert* v *United States Government* (5). It should also be noted in this problem that the conspiracy, while initiated outside the jurisdiction, would have to be effected in State K, ie the overthrow of the government.

The effects doctrine and the protective principle are often treated as one and the same, and it is often difficult to determine which category a situation falls into. Some decided cases fit uneasily into either of the two categories. In *Attorney-General of the Government of Israel* v *Eichmann* (6) the State of Israel argued, inter alia, that it had jurisdiction to try the accused on the basis that his actions were prejudicial to the State of Israel, although the State was not in existence at the time of his crimes.

State K might also invoke the passive personality principle, in that the potential victims of the crime (presuming that K citizens would have been killed or injured in the overthrow) were nationals of State K even though the crime was in the main part committed abroad. The nationality of Fernandez is, of course, irrelevant to the above claims of jurisdiction. The passive personality claim of jurisdiction is not accepted by all States and it would depend upon the attitude of courts of State K. In *United States* v *Yunis* (7) the court, contrary to previous practice, accepted this principle, although as the case involved air piracy and the taking of hostages it had a universal application.

State K would, of course, be in a much stronger position if the planned crime had been executed. The State could then rely upon the territorial principle giving it jurisdiction over crimes committed within its territory. In this instance, where the conspiracy was plotted abroad, State K would be able to claim jurisdiction under the objective territorial principle if the crime was completed within its jurisdiction.

State M will seek to claim jurisdiction over Fernandez on the basis of nationality. A State may prosecute its nationals for crimes committed anywhere in the world. It will, however, depend on the law of State M as to which crimes have extra-territorial effect. In the United Kingdom, for instance, reserves the right to prosecute its nationals for murder, bigamy, treason, crimes against humanity and war crimes. If the laws of State M make it an extra-territorial crime to engage in a conspiracy to overthrow a foreign government then State M may claim jurisdiction on this basis.

One is told that Fernandez is a national of State M currently residing in State L. For a State to offer diplomatic protection to one of its nationals, that is to intervene internationally on their behalf, there must be 'a genuine connection'. This was discussed in the *Nottehohm Case: Liechtenstein* v *Guatemala* (8) in which the ICJ stated that there must be 'a legal bond having as its basis a social fact of attachment, a genuine connection of existence ...'.

For State M to challenge the workings of the courts of State L and to seek the extradition of Fernandez to State M his nationality must be established. It is submitted that although he lives in State L Fernandez has not in any way abrogated his State M nationality and therefore State M may pursue his extradition. It is, however, unlikely to succeed because State M's argument as to the harsh treatment Fernandez will receive is unlikely to find favour in the courts of State L, unless there is a bi-lateral treaty designed to safeguard the treatment and rights of those being held. In issues of concurrent jurisdiction where more than one State has jurisdiction priority to exercise enforcement jurisdiction depends upon custody.

References

(1) *Preliminary Objections* (1962) ICJ Rep p319; *Second Phase* (1966) ICJ Rep p6

(2) (1974) ICJ Rep pp253 and 457

(3) (1957) ICJ Rep p9

(4) [1991] 2 QB 130

(5) [1991] 1 AC 225

(6) (1961) 36 ILR 5

(7) (1988) 681 F Supp 896; (1989) 83 AJIL 94

(8) (1955) ICJ Rep p4

QUESTION 4

a) 'The Vienna Convention on Diplomatic Relations, 1961, requires radical revision.'

Discuss.

b) State A's authorities suspect that Edvard, a member of the staff of State B's diplomatic mission to State A, is engaged in drug smuggling activities. Assuming that both States are parties to the Vienna Convention on Diplomatic Relations, 1961, advise State A's authorities as to whether they may:

   i) subject the diplomatic bag of State B to electronic surveillance;

   ii) search the private residence of Edvard and of his driver, Maria, who is a national of State A;

   iii) arrest Edvard and Maria when they attend a meeting with suspected drug dealers outside the capital of State A; and

   iv) expel the ambassador of State B for failing to prevent the alleged drug smuggling activities.

SUGGESTED SOLUTION TO QUESTION 4

General Comment

The question is neatly divided up into two sections. The answer to part (a) may be utilised to help answer the problems presented in part (b).

Part (a) invites a discussion of the main areas of diplomatic immunity relating to the misuse of diplomatic missions, of personal diplomatic immunity and of the diplomatic bag. The answer should also include a defence of the Vienna Convention and the importance of diplomatic immunity in the international system.

Skeleton Solution

a) Introduction – status of Vienna Convention.

   Abuse of the functions of a foreign embassy – Libya and Sun Yat Sen incidents.

   Actions of diplomatic staff.

   Diplomatic bag and its misuse.

   Conclusion and necessity of diplomatic immunity.

b) i) Article 27(3) Vienna Convention.

   ii) Article 30 and private residence of diplomats.

   Status of private residence of service staff.

   iii) Article 26 and freedom of movement.

   Immunity from arrest of categories of staff.

   iv) Persona non grata and workings of art 9.

Suggested Solution

a) The Vienna Convention codified the rules on diplomatic immunity. More than 150 states have ratified it and it is recognised as being in accordance with customary international law. It can therefore be used as evidence of customary international law even in situations involving a State which is not party to the convention.

   Diplomatic immunity was a feature of the ancient Greek

system of city States and is regarded as 'essential for the relations between states as accepted by nations of all creeds and political complexions': *United States Diplomatic and Consular Staff in Tehran Case* (1). Diplomatic representation and diplomatic relations are not a requirement in international law but the vast majority of states have some form of diplomatic representation abroad and receive diplomats on their territory.

Why, then, is there a demand that the Vienna Convention be fundamentally redrawn? The disquiet with the Convention and its workings originates in the abuse of the diplomatic norms by some States. Article 3 of the Convention outlines the main functions of a diplomatic mission and these involve representation of the sending State, protection of its interests and nationals and, importantly, the promotion of friendly relations. This not always the case. A foreign embassy may involve itself in actions which are hostile to the interests of the receiving State. The most notable example of this took place in London on 17 April 1984 during a peaceful demonstration outside the Libyan Embassy. Shots were fired from the Embassy at a group of demonstrators opposed to the government of Libya. One of the shots killed a policewoman who was marshalling the demonstrators. Following this event the United Kingdom ordered the closure of the Libyan Embassy and the expulsion of her diplomats. The Embassy staff and organisation were obviously not involved in promoting friendly relations between Britain and Libya, but the receiving State was unable to vet the activities of the embassy. Similarly, in the Sun Yat San incident a Chinese national was kidnapped and held against his will in the Chinese Embassy. Although the British government expressed its displeasure to the government of China the court in the United Kingdom refused to intervene.

It is, however, with the activities of diplomatic staff outside their embassy that most disquiet has been expressed. Diplomatic agents have complete immunity from the criminal jurisdiction of the receiving State and immunity from the civil jurisdiction save in respect of, inter alia, actions relating to private real property or succession under a will. A diplomat is therefore immune from the criminal law in relation to, for example, murder or theft. Abuses of this immunity have been a cause for concern. Parking offences in London are the most common examples of errant behaviour but diplomats have also indulged in other areas. Dixon (2) quotes the statistic that in 1996 29 diplomats were found to be responsible for 'serious offences'. The receiving State may of course exercise its discretion and declare the diplomat 'persona non grata', but what it cannot do is punish the diplomat. Article 41 places an obligation on diplomats to obey the receiving State's laws, but by the same article the receiving State is prevented from interfering with the privileges and immunities of the diplomat. The only option open to the receiving State is either to utilise art 32 and ask for the diplomat's immunity to be waived or else, as mentioned above, declare the individual persona non grata. Administrative and technical staff also enjoy immunities similar to the diplomatic staff with the exception that their civil immunity is limited to their official duties: art 37(2). Such individuals are therefore free to engage in potentially unlawful activities in the receiving State. The most common example during the cold war was, of course, spying.

Under art 27 the receiving State is obliged to protect free communications for all official purposes and the sending State is authorised to use codes to communicate with its home State. The receiving State is also forbidden to open or detain the diplomatic bag: art 27(3). The image of the diplomatic bag is, however, at variance with the reality, and it may consist of large wooden crates rather than a hand-held bag. As long as the item has visible external marks identifying it as a diplomatic bag it cannot be opened or detained. This aspect of diplomatic immunity has been the subject of much debate owing to its misuse for the smuggling of drugs or even in the case of Nigeria, people (3). Dikko, a former Nigerian government Minister was kidnapped by Nigerian agents, drugged and placed in a crate, a diplomatic bag, destined for Nigeria. The crate was examined following insufficient official paperwork and was found to contain Dikko and his kidnappers. The United Kingdom government justified this breach of diplomatic protocol on the basis that a receiving State is entitled so to do where there is a threat to an individual's wellbeing.

Against this background diplomatic immunity, or its extent, has been called into question, particularly in relation to the diplomatic bag. The United Kingdom, for instance, would like to have the authority to open the bag in the presence of an official of the embassy and if this is refused then to have the authority to order the return of the bag to the sending State. However, certain countries have given a flexible interpretation of when they may violate diplomatic premises or hinder the workings of a diplomatic mission. In 1984 following the closure of the Libyan Embassy the building was searched by the British police in the presence of a Saudi diplomat. This would appear to be in breach of art 45(a) which states that after a break in diplomatic relations 'the receiving State must ... respect and protect the premises of the mission'. The United Kingdom argued that does not mean that the premises continue to be inviolable, and one may argue that the search could be justified as a right of self-defence.

It is, however, when the consequences of abandoning diplomatic immunity are considered that the present system looks most satisfactory. The invasion and seizure of the hostages in the American Embassy in Tehran provide a vivid example of the dangers (4), as does the possibility of diplomats being arrested on false charges.

b) i) Under art 27 the receiving State is obliged to permit and protect free communications for all official purposes. The diplomatic mission may, however, only install and use a wireless transmitter with the consent of the receiving State: art 27(1). State A may therefore be using an electronic surveillance system in order to ascertain whether the diplomatic bag contains a wireless transmitter. If State B has no permission to use a wireless transmitter and is so doing then State A is justified in complaining to State B. What is not permissible is to open or detain the diplomatic bag to confirm or refute this belief.

ii) Whether a search of the private residence of Edvard is permitted would depend upon his status. One is only told that he is a member of staff.

If Edvard is a diplomatic agent then his private residence is inviolable: art 30. The private residence enjoys the same inviolability as the diplomatic mission. This also true of the diplomatic agent's papers. If Edvard is a member of the administrative and technical staff then similar immunities will apply as long as he is not a national of State A nor permanently resident in State A. However, Maria is a national of State A so even if she is classed as technical and administrative staff she will attract no immunity to her residence which will not be inviolable.

Equally, no immunity will apply to Maria's residence if she is a member of the service staff or a private servant, which is likely in the case of a driver.

iii) Edvard is permitted to journey outside the capital of State A. Under art 26 the receiving Sate is obliged to ensure freedom of movement for all members of the mission provided the area is not a prohibited zone which is designated as such on grounds of national security.

The arrest of Edvard will not be lawful if he is a diplomatic agent; that is if he is head of the mission or a member of the diplomatic staff of the mission. A diplomatic agent is completely immune from the criminal jurisdiction of the receiving state (art 31) and cannot be detained. If Edvard is a member of the administrative and technical staff, for example a clerk or radio operator, he will also enjoy complete immunity from criminal jurisdiction: art 37(2). If he is a member of the service staff he will enjoy immunity only in respect of acts performed in the course of his duties: art 37(3). The meeting with suspected drug dealers is unlikely to fall into this category.

As a national of State A and presumably a member of the service staff or a private servant, Maria will enjoy no immunities: art 37(3) and (4).

iv) The ambassador may be declared persona non grata by State A. If this happens, he should either be recalled by State B or have his functions with the mission terminated: art 9. State A is not obliged to furnish any explanation when notifying State B of its decision to declare a member of State B's diplomatic staff persona non grata. If State B refuses or fails to carry out its resulting obligations then State A may refuse to recognise the ambassador as a member of the mission: art 9(2).

References

(1) (1980) ICJ Rep 3

(2) *International Law* (3rd ed), p182

(3) Discussed in (1985) 34 ICLQ 602

(4) See (1980) ICJ Rep 3 (Reference (1) above)

QUESTION 5

The population of the State of Despairia consists of two ethnic groups, the Wabenzi, who make up 60 per cent of the population and who control the government and the armed forces, and the Ba-Audi, who comprise the remaining 40 per cent. After an outbreak of unrest amongst the Ba-Audi minority, many Ba-Audi have been arrested and their villages burned by government troops. The situation has provoked a mass exodus of Ba-Audi refugees into the neighbouring state of Zenubia, causing there major economic problems and a breakdown of law and order.

Zenubia has approached the Security Council of the United Nations, asking for authority to intervene in Despairia in order to enforce the establishment of a protected zone for the Ba-Audi people. The government of Despairia has warned that any intervention within its territory would amount to a flagrant breach of fundamental principles of international law as incorporated in the United Nations Charter.

Advise Zenubia as to:

a) how the Security Council is likely to respond to Zenubia's request; and

b) whether, in the event of no action being taken by the Security Council, international law entitles Zenubia to intervene unilaterally?

SUGGESTED SOLUTION TO QUESTION 5

General Comment

This problem requires an understanding of the power and functions of the Security Council with reference to intervention and the use of force in the affairs of another State. The candidate should be aware of customary international law and the provisions of the UN Charter in relation to State sovereignty and the use of force. In addition, an acquaintance with the doctrine of humanitarian intervention is necessary to answer part (b).

Skeleton Solution

a) State sovereignty; art 2(7).
   Power and functions of Security Council.
   Iraq and Somalia precedents.
   Workings of Ch VII.

b) Article 2(4).
   Article 51.
   Humanitarian intervention.
   Conclusion.

Suggested Solution

a) The presumption of international law is against interference in the domestic affairs of a State. International law on the relationship between States is based on the principle of sovereign equality between States. The origin of this principle may be found in the Peace Treaty of Westphalia (1648). The notion of sovereign equality means that all States have equal rights and duties. All States are entitled to exercise exclusive jurisdiction over their domestic affairs, and no one State may intervene in the domestic affairs of another.

   The modern reiteration of this principle is found in the UN Charter, which recognises sovereign equality – the Security Council notwithstanding – and which states in art 2(7):

> 'Nothing contained in the present Charter shall authorise the UN to intervene in matters which are essentially within the domestic jurisdiction of any state'.

The Security Council may, however, effectively override these provisions if the consequences of the domestic affairs of a State threaten international peace and security. By art 24 the Security Council is given primary responsibility for the maintenance of international peace and security. The Council has first to determine any threat to international peace and then once that determination is made in accordance with art 39 the Council may act. What amounts to a threat to international peace and security of the world community is not defined in the UN Charter. It is for the Council to determine as each situation presents itself.

Zenubia could argue that there are precedents supporting UN action in the internal affairs of other States. The most relevant precedent is to be found in Security Council Resolution 688 which was passed in the aftermath of the Gulf War. The failure of the Kurdish revolt against the Iraqi regime resulted in a mass exodus of Iraqi Kurds (an ethnic minority) into the neighbouring States of Iran and, principally, Turkey. The actions of the Iraqi government were condemned by the UN and measures were instituted to protect the Kurdish minority in the north of the country. The mass exodus of refugees was deemed to have a destabilising effect on the region and was thus a matter of concern to the Security Council in its role of sentinel of international peace and security. The situation in Despairia is somewhat similar. The mass exodus of Ba-Audi refugees has caused considerable internal problems to Zenubia.

Zenubia will also find a precedent in UN actions in Somalia. Security Council Res 794 authorised a United States force to intervene in Somalia with the proviso that they report their actions to the Security Council. The purpose of the force was to restore order to the disintegrated state of Somalia and 'to speed food and medical supplies to the ... victims of drought and civil war' (President Bush). The justification for this action was humanitarian as there was little evidence that the civil war in Somalia was having a significant effect in destabilising the region. Zenubia could, however, cite this precedent, as presumably one of the reasons it wishes to establish a protected zone for the Ba-Audi people is because of their harsh treatment by the government of Despairia. While the UN Security Council authorised action in Bosnia may provide a superficial precedent it should be pointed out that Bosnia, a recognised State, invited the UN and then the IFOR troops into its jurisdiction. Moreover Zenubia's possible reference to these precedents is only useful as a means of persuasion, because the Security Council is not bound by its own decisions. In addition, the Security Council is only as active or inaction as the Member States, and particularly the Permanent Members, wish it to be. Under art 27 decisions of the Council must be made by an affirmative vote of nine members including the votes of the Permanent Members. An abstention by a Permanent Member is not, however, treated as a veto.

Zenubia, it should be noted, has asked for authority to intervene in Despairia rather than asking for UN troops to intervene. Under Ch VII art 42 the UN is authorised to use force to maintain international peace and security and the UN is permitted to delegate its functions to Member States provided they are authorised by the UN. In the Korean War the Security Council passed a resolution recommending that Member States send forces to help South Korea. This was passed under the terms of art 39 and the result was a UN force under the command of the US President. Zenubia's forces could therefore 'wear the blue helmet' but be under the control of the Zenubian government. UN authority to act is the key to understanding the legal justification: without the UN authority to act the legal justification is much more limited (see below). A different situation arose in the Gulf War where by Res 678 the Security Council authorised Member States, co-operating with the government of Kuwait, to use all necessary means to restore international peace and security in the area. The Gulf War coalition was not composed of UN troops, rather they were UN-authorised troops. Similarly the no-fly zones over Iraq are UN-authorised but enforced by the United States, the United Kingdom and France. Zenubia is therefore perfectly entitled to ask for authority to intervene in Despairia but whether this is granted or not is a separate matter.

b) Zenubia's entitlement to act unilaterally is much more open to question. Article 2(4) of the Charter states:

> 'All members shall refrain ... from the use of force against ... the political independence of any State'.

Zenubia is also prohibited from infringing the territorial integrity of other States. This view is supported in customary international law and repeated in *Nicaragua* v *United States (Merits)* (1).

How, then, may Zenubia make out a case for intervention?

Zenubia could argue that it is entitled to intervene on the grounds of self-defence. The mass exodus of Ba-Audi refugees has caused a severe disruption to its domestic situation. Under art 51 a State is entitled to use force for the purposes of self-defence. What amounts to self-defence is not defined in the article, perhaps deliberately so, and has been a cause of contention. In 1972 India intervened in the civil war raging in East Pakistan arguing that its territorial integrity and security was being threatened by the mass exodus of people from East Pakistan to West Bengal. Such a justification was not without controversy because the move resulted in the defect of the Pakistani army and the establishment of the State of Bangladesh.

If Zenubia were to plead self-defence then the action must be limited to the threat and have no ulterior purpose. The 'action taken must not be unreasonable or excessive': *Caroline Case* (2). The situation must also leave no other choice. This is not the case here because the Security Council has chosen *not* to act rather than being *unable* to act.

Brownlie (3) argues that a State may not empower itself to intervene, by force, unilaterally in the affairs of another State. The custodian of the international legal system is the UN and in particular the Security Council. The contrary view, supporting the right to self-defence if the UN fails to act, is supported by such legal writers as Bowett and Lillich.

One is told that the Ba-Audi do not control the government and the armed forces. They have also been treated harshly, having their villages burned and being subjected to what appears to be mass arrest. Such a situation may support the contention of Zenubia that it is entitled to intervene on humanitarian grounds.

Humanitarian intervention was a doctrine espoused particularly in the nineteenth century and which provided the legal justification of one State to forcibly intervene in the affairs of another. The origins of the rule may be found, inter alia, in the writings of Vattel and Grotius, who adhered to the view that if a ruler was abusing the rights of his subjects then intervention was justified. France, for instance, intervened in the nineteenth century to protect the rights of the Christian population in what is now Lebanon. Whether this is applicable today is open to question. As with the right of self-defence, the legal justification of a State to act unilaterally must be examined in the light of the functions of the Security Council. Even where the Security

Council has taken actions which are akin to humanitarian intervention, as in Somalia, it has seen fit to put in a caveat. The preamble to Security Council Res 794 in relation to Somalia talks about the 'unique character of Somalia' as one of the justifications for allowing the UN and United States troops into the country for humanitarian purposes. This phrase was inserted to calm third-world fears about the resurrection of humanitarian intervention. While India's action in East Pakistan (see above) looked to have the character of humanitarian intervention, India was careful to argue self-defence. Rather than being entitled to intervene, Zenubia may find itself condemned by the Security Council.

References

(1) (1986) ICJ Rep p14
(2) (1837) 29 BFSP 1137
(3) *Principles of Public International Law* (4th ed 1990)

QUESTION 6

To what extent do individuals possess procedural capacity in global and regional regimes established for the protection of human rights?

SUGGESTED SOLUTION TO QUESTION 6

General Comment

This is a rather narrow question which involves an analysis of the various procedural devices by which an individual may raise the issue of human rights violations and possibly seek compensation. The candidate should be familiar with the main international and regional treaties in this area. In addition knowledge of the avenues available before UN committees and commissions is needed.

Skeleton Solution

Introduction – theory of the individual as a subject in international law.

UN Charter and the human rights provisions therein – UDHR.

First Optional Protocol, Civil and Political Covenant and workings thereof.

UN Commission on Human Rights: Res 1503.

ECHR – art 25 and the workings thereof – art 26.

American Convention on Human Rights.

Conclusion.

Suggested Solution

The traditional theory of international law from the time of the Peace of Westphalia (1648) until the end of the 1914–18 war subscribed to the view that only States were subjects of international law. This standpoint has, however, been challenged since the end of the 1914–18 War. Under the 'minority treaties' enacted under the umbrella of the 1919 Peace Agreement individuals were given standing and in its Advisory Opinion relating to the *Danzig Postal Service* (1) the Permanent Court of International Justice (PCIJ) stated that there was nothing in international law to prevent individuals from being granted rights under a treaty.

It was with the end of the Second World War that individuals were granted a significant increase in the number of instances in which they could initiate proceedings in order to protect their rights. This was, however, a gradual process and at first the UN contented itself with establishing international standards for the protection of human rights. Reference to the concept of human rights is found in the UN Charter. The Preamble to the Charter states that the Peoples of the UN reaffirm their 'faith in fundamental human rights ... in the equal rights of men and women'. Article 1(3) of the Charter lists among the main purposes of the UN the achievement of international cooperation:

> 'In promoting and encouraging respect for human rights and for fundamental freedoms for all without distinction as to race, sex, language or religion'.

Article 55 States that the UN shall promote:

> 'Universal respect for and observance of human rights and fundamental freedoms for all without distinction as to race, sex, language or religion.'

Article 56 talks about members of the UN pledging themselves to take joint and separate action in co-operation with the organisation to achieve the purposes set out in art 55.

Further, the Universal Declaration of Human Rights (UDHR) set out a 'charter' of those rights which it was hoped would be respected by the world community. It was a standard-setting document and was not intended to be legally binding. The Member States of the UN were reluctant to establish any enforcement mechanisms for the protection of human rights and moreover the Soviet Union and the countries of the 'Eastern Bloc' denied that individuals were subjects of international law. Any procedural capacity of individuals in this area, the Soviet Union argued, would be a violation of national sovereignty and would conflict with art 2(7) of the UN charter which forbids intervention in the domestic affairs of States.

The UN therefore proceeded cautiously in this area and separated the issue of putative individual capacity from that of standard setting and inter-state complaints. The International Covenant of 1966 on Civil and Political Rights reflects this approach. The First *Optional* Protocol to the Civil and Political Covenant is just that. This is a separate document and requires separate ratification from the Covenant. The Protocol establishes the procedure whereby an individual may make a complaint to the 18-person Human Rights Committee (HRC) established under the Covenant. The individual will have to make out a case that his/her rights as set out in the Covenant have been violated: if this is not the case then the application may be declared inadmissible. The individual has to comply with the requirement of exhausting local remedies, which is a standard requirement before international proceedings are initiated: *Ambatielos Arbitration* (2).

The international procedure is not, however, comparable to an individual bringing a case before a domestic tribunal, as the Human Rights Committee is not a court and it has no power to compel the allegedly errant State to appear or to provide the necessary documentation. Further, any decision that the Committee may reach does not bind the State. Thus the individual has procedural capacity to bring his case before the Committee if the State so wishes and has ratified the Optional Protocol, but that does not guarantee any resolution of the action.

The UN has also attempted to put in place other means of human rights enforcement (in the broad sense of the word) to assist the individual. This has been initiated by means of investigation and reporting without the necessity of a State having had to ratify a treaty or covenant. Since 1971 the Commission on Human Rights has been able to debate complaints submitted to it by the Sub-Commission on Prevention of Discrimination and Protection of Minorities. The Sub-Commission is authorised by Res 1503 to form a working group to examine individual petitions relating to violations of human rights received by the Secretary General of the UN, and to then report to the Sub-Commission the violations which appear to reveal a 'consistent pattern of gross and reliably attested violations of human rights'. Reference on to the Commission could then follow. Whether or not this is a worthwhile procedure for the individual to follow is open to question. The standards of application of this procedure have not been universal and any attempt to introduce alternative procedures other than judicial or even quasi-judicial raises an issue of political pressure.

The regional picture, at least in Europe, is much more satisfactory. By art 25 the European Convention on Human Rights entitles the European Commission on Human Rights to receive petitions from individuals. Firstly the Commission must decide whether the petition is admissible. The individual must be a victim. The applicant cannot complain of a violation to which he is a 'stranger'. This issue was discussed in *Dudgeon* (3) in which the applicant, a United Kingdom citizen resident in Northern Ireland, was subject to a police search of his flat for evidence relating to illegal possession of drugs. When lawfully present in his flat they seized material concerning his homosexual activities (then a criminal offence in Northern Ireland). The police returned the material and decided not to prosecute. He nevertheless convinced the Court (ECHR), by a majority, that the possibility of a prosecution for homosexual activities made him a victim, although no prosecutions had been brought in the immediate years proceeding this case.

The victim must also have exhausted all domestic remedies (art 26), a requirement which is relatively easy to fulfil as regards the United Kingdom because the absence of a Bill of Rights means that the issue may be conclusively dealt with by a court of first instance.

The majority of cases brought before the Commission are, however, declared inadmissible as they do not raise an issue within the terms of the European Convention or the matter is substantially the same as a matter which has already been examined by the Commission: art 27(1)(b). Moreover, only States or the Commission may refer a case to the Court: art 44. It is, however, proposed that individuals will have the right to bring a case before the Court. It should be stressed though that the capacity of the individual to bring a case before the Commission and the subsequent hearings by the Court has provided a stronger impetus to the development of the jurisprudence of the Convention than the inter-State procedure.

Those States which have ratified the European Convention cannot opt out of the inter-State complaint procedure but may choose *not* to make an optional declaration allowing individual petition, while the reverse is true with the American Convention on Human Rights. On ratification of the American Convention the States agree to the compulsory nature of the individual petition procedure whereby the matter is dealt with by the Inter-American Commission of Human Rights. The jurisdiction of the Courts is, however, optional and, as with all treaties, the rights of the individual (whether substantive or procedural) depend upon whether the State concerned wishes to ratify the treaty in the first place.

The trend in international human rights organisations and even international institutions with a wider brief is to grant individuals locus standi in matters concerning the interpretation of their rights under a treaty. The European Council, for instance, proposed in Protocol 11 to make a citizen's direct right of appeal mandatory, thereby allowing automatic access to the European Court of Human Rights, while the UN Human Rights Commission and its Sub-Commission have been active in hearing allegations from individuals which allegedly show 'widespread and serious human rights abuses'. All the above should nevertheless be treated with caution – individuals are not tenants in the international legal system but rather licencees functioning by the largesse of States and institutions.

References

(1) (1925) PCIJ Rep Series B No 11
(2) *Greece* v *United Kingdom* (1956) 12 RIAA 83
(3) [1981] 4 EHRR 149

QUESTION 7

a) Why was the incorporation of the concept of jus cojens into the Vienna Convention on the Law of Treaties, 1961, a source of controversy?

b) In 1996, Arcadia, a former colony of Imperia, obtained independence after a long struggle for national liberation. The new foreign minister of Arcadia seeks your advice on the following matters:

   i) Arcadia's obligations, if any, in respect of a treaty concluded in 1982 by Imperia under which a substantial part of the then colony of Arcadia was transferred to the neighbouring state of Sindaria in return for military assistance against the Arcadian Liberation Front;

   ii) Arcadia's wish to become a party to a United Nations Convention on Compulsory Dispute Settlement subject to a reservation excluding disputes with Imperia in respect of any matters arising before Arcadia's independence.

SUGGESTED SOLUTION TO QUESTION 7

General Comment

A question divided into three parts, the first section of which invites a discussion of the meaning of jus cogens. Because there is no definitive answer, this answers the question as to why its incorporation was a source of controversy.

The remaining parts of the question relate to the issue of jus cogens in seeking a solution to the problems. The issue of self-determination and its possible inclusion as a peremptory norm of international law needs to be discussed.

Part (b)(ii) includes a consideration of reservations to treaties and the Vienna Convention on the Succession of States in Respect of Treaties 1978.

The writer has assumed that 1961 is a misprint as the Vienna Convention on the Law of Treaties is 1969.

Skeleton Solution

a) Jus cogens and peremptory norms – where do they come from? What are they?

   Moral content of law.

   Conclusion.

b) i) Self-determination – the importance of the rule.

   The source of self-determination.

   The relationship to the problem.

   ii) Significance of reservations.

   Vienna Convention Treaties – *Genocide Case.*

   Vienna Convention on Succession of States.

   Conclusion.

Suggested Solution

a) Jus cogens refers to the body of peremptory norms of international law. Being peremptory no derogation from them is permitted and any derogation will involve the treaty being declared invalid.

Article 53 of the Vienna Convention 1969 defines a peremptory norm of international law as:

> 'a norm accepted and recognised by the international community of States ... and which can be modified only by a subsequent norm of general international law having the same character.'

Article 64 of the Vienna Convention goes on to say:

> 'If a new peremptory norm of general international law emerges, any existing treaty which is in conflict with that norm becomes void and terminates.'

Such is the effect of violating a norm of international law. What is less clear is what amounts to a peremptory norm and where do they originate? Article 64 talks about peremptory norms 'emerging', which would indicate that they might come from customary law, only being deemed to exist once the world community of States has accepted them. They might also originate from a treaty which has received universal approval or, more likely, a treaty which has served to codify customary international law, the Vienna Convention on Diplomatic Relations 1961 being an example.

Peremptory norms may emerge from a UN General Assembly Resolution which has been passed by a large majority with no votes against it, the Universal Declaration of Human Rights and Res 1514 on the Granting of Independence to Colonial Peoples being examples – their passage may have resulted in peremptory norms of human rights and self-determination for peoples (1). The problem with this area of international law is that not only is the definition of a peremptory norm unclear, (for example, who constitute 'peoples' entitled to self-determination?), but also may a definitive list of such norms be drawn up at any one time?

It is submitted that there are now a limited number of peremptory norms of international law such as the prohibitions on the slave trade and piracy. It is easy to predict that a treaty authorising either would be void as both constitute international crimes. Other examples of the same genre which have emerged in the post-war era include the possibility of a treaty to effect genocide (the prohibition thereof being found in a treaty: Convention on the Prevention and Punishment of the Crime of Genocide (1948)) and a treaty which might involve crimes against humanity.

Other areas are more opaque. The principle of non-discrimination on the grounds of race and the prohibition of racial discrimination might possibly be categorised as a norm of international law. It has not, however, been suggested that the treaty between the United Kingdom and the People's Republic of China be declared void, even though the treaty takes into account ethnic origins in determining who is entitled to Chinese citizenship after 1997.

It has been argued that the

> 'rules of jus cogens will encompass rules based more on "morality" or "natural law" than the traditionalist "positivist" rules' (2).

As such they can be hard to define, and supporting the contention that a treaty is against jus cogens introduces an element of uncertainty into international practice and jurisprudence.

b) i) In its former status of a colony of Imperia, Arcadia was denied the right to self-determination. This right is referred to in art 1(2) of the UN Charter which states that one of the organisation's purposes is to develop friendly relations among nations based upon respect for the principle of equal rights and self-determination. Article 55 of the Charter also makes reference to self-determination, as do the International 'Human Rights' Covenants 1966. Moreover, Res 1514 might be a contributory factor in this area (3). Judicial discussion of the principle of self-determination is found in the *Namibia Advisory Opinion* (4) and the *Western Sahara Case: Advisory Opinion* (5).

It is against this background that we must consider the contention that the 1982 treaty represents a rule of jus cogens. The treaty between Imperia and Sindaria would appear to violate the right of self-determination for the people of Arcadia. The doctrine of self-determination is designed to facilitate the independence of colonial peoples within already existing colonial boundaries. This is not the case here, and in fact the treaty appears to be designed to thwart the wishes of the people of Arcadia in that the neighbouring State of Sindaria has helped in the suppression of the Arcadian Liberation Front. Further, while the act of secession is not against international law it presumably will be an expression of self-determination, which is not the situation in this case. An act of secession is permissible in international law but in this case a substantial part of Arcadia was transferred to the State of Sindaria by Imperia without the consent of the Arcadian population. A substantial part of Arcadia was transferred by the colonial power, without, one would surmise, the consent of the population of Arcadia.

Arcadia should be advised that the treaty is in violation of jus cogens and will not be valid. It is void from its inception.

ii) It is permissible in international law to enter a reservation concerning a treaty. A reservation is defined in art 2 Vienna Convention on the Law of Treaties as a statement by a State which purports to 'exclude or to modify the legal effect of certain provisions of the treaty in their application to that State'.

The significance of a reservation was discussed in an Advisory Opinion of the ICJ in *Reservations to the Convention on Genocide Case* (6). The Court was of the opinion that

> 'a State may be regarded as being a party to the Convention if the reservation is compatible with the object and purposes of the Convention.'

What is or is not compatible with the Convention is, according to the *Genocide Case*, to be decided by States individually. The effect of this in practice means that a State may be a party to the treaty in the eyes of some States but not of others.

Articles 19–21 of the Vienna Convention follow the opinion in the *Genocide Case*, except in cases where by art 20(2)

> 'it appears from the limited number of States and the object and purpose of the treaty that the application of the treaty in its entirety between all the parties is an essential condition of the consent of each one to be bound by the treaty'.

In this instance it is most unlikely that only a limited number of States would become a party to a UN Convention.

Arcadia will be seen in international law as the successor to Imperia over its territory. The standard rule is that 'new' or recently independent States are not bound by treaties made on their behalf by the former sovereign or colonial power. This is put forth in the Vienna Convention on the Succession of States in Respect of Treaties 1978. There is an exception, however, in relation to boundaries. Articles 11 and 12 of the Succession Convention cover boundaries and provide that territorial boundaries are binding on the new State.

Arcadia should therefore be advised that she is not bound by any treaty altering her territory as this goes against a rule of jus cogens, namely self-determination. The territorial question is likely to be the main item of dispute with

Imperia. Arcadia should enter a reservation in case of any other disputes with Imperia, but the dispute over the transfer of territory should not be part of Arcadia's reservation as any agency established under the said UN Convention on Dispute Settlement is likely to rule in favour Arcadia that the treaty between Imperia and Sindaria is against a rule of jus cogens and therefore void.

References

(1) See also the Suggested Solution to Question 1 for a further discussion of this area

(2) Dixon *International Law* (3rd ed), p68

(3) See comments above in part (a) and in the Suggested Solution to Question 1

(4) *Legal Consequences for States of the Continued Presence of South Africa in Namibia (South West Africa) Case* (1971) ICJ Rep p6

(5) (1975) ICJ Rep p12

(6) (1951) ICJ Rep p15

QUESTION 8

GTZ is a public limited company incorporated in State S which owns 51 per cent of Cidecorp, an arms manufacturing company incorporated under the laws of State T. Recently, Cidecorp sold an anti-aircraft missile system to the Beta Liberation Movement (BLM), an organisation which seeks independence for the people residing in the Beta region of State U. When the BTM ordered the missile system, it made no secret of its intention to use the missiles against State U's military aircraft. Three days after the missile system was installed, it was used to shoot down a reconnaissance aircraft belonging to the State U airforce, resulting in the deaths of six members of the crew and of four military advisers from State V.

Prepare a memorandum considering any claims that might arise in international law in respect of the deaths.

SUGGESTED SOLUTION TO QUESTION 8

General Comment

This question involves consideration of a number of different issues. Firstly the problem of how to determine the State nationality of a company needs to be addressed. Is it the jurisdiction where the company is incorporated or the State of effective control? Having discussed this problem (there is no definitive answer) the candidate should examine the issue of State responsibility, if any, for public corporations and whether the actions of a corporation may be imputed to a State.

If imputability is accepted then a discussion is required of the objective and fault theories of State responsibility. A firm answer as to which theory should apply is not possible. Finally, a summary of the remedies available in international law for such an event is useful.

Skeleton Solution

Companies in international law.

State nationality of companies – how this is determined.

State responsibility for entities with a 'genuine connection' to the State.

State authority and control over these entities.

State responsibility, objective and fault theory: *Corfu Channel Case; Home Missionaries Claim.*

Remedies.

Conclusion.

Suggested Solution

The position of companies in international law presents a number of problems. When a company suffers at the hands of another State this may give rise to an issue of State responsibility. The company is not normally a party to the international proceedings and international law has to determine which State is the State of nationality of the company. When this is determined the State concerned may offer diplomatic protection to the company and intervene on the company's behalf. The usual method of determining the nationality of a company is to see where the company has its registered office, ie where the company was incorporated. This is not necessarily the same as the nationality of the shareholders but if damage is done to the company it is the State of nationality of the company which is deemed to have suffered rather than the State of which the shareholders are nationals: *Barcelona Traction, Light and Power Co Case: Belgium* v *Spain* (1).

The above may not, however, according with reality. The State where the company is incorporated may not reflect the State in which the actual control of the company is.

The control of a company may be ascertained by seeing where the majority of shares are held. If the majority of the shares are held in a different jurisdiction from where the company is incorporated then the former jurisdiction may provide the State of nationality of the company. In the problem GTZ, a public limited company incorporated in State S, owns 51 per cent of Cidecorp, a company incorporated in State T. GTZ would therefore have a controlling interest in Cidecorp and State S may be regarded in international law as being the State of nationality of Cidecorp.

Whether the test is the State of incorporation or the State of effective control, only one State may be the State of nationality. The general consensus would, however, be in the direction of where the company is incorporated rather than where the control is exercised. Dixon (2) quotes the United States–Iran Claims Settlement Declaration 1981 as evidence of a compromise solution to the problem. In that example, for either Iran or the United States to have locus standi to bring a claim in respect of a company, the company had to be incorporated in the State and a majority of the shareholders had to be nationals of that State.

In this instance one is not confronted with an injury suffered by a company but rather the question of whether the State of nationality of the company will be held responsible for the deaths of the nationals of States U and V and the loss of the aircraft belonging to State U.

State responsibility is a fundamental principle of international law and any 'breach of an engagement involves an obligation to make reparations': *Chorzow Factory Case (Indemnity) (Merits): Germany* v *Poland* (3).

A State is only liable for its own actions or omissions rather than for its population as a whole. The question to consider in this instance is whether either State S or State T is responsible for the actions of Cidecorp in selling the anti-aircraft missile system and whether the subsequent deaths and injuries are the responsibility of either State or none.

The general rule relating to acts of private persons is stated in art 11 International Law Commission (ILC) Draft Articles:

> 'The conduct of a person or a group of persons *not* acting on behalf of the State shall not be considered as an act of the State under international law.'

The ILC did, however, go on to discuss the position of entities or persons who though not organs of the State or State officials nevertheless have a genuine connection with State activities. In para 2 of draft art 7 it is stated:

> 'The conduct of an organ of an entity which is not part of the formal structure of the State or of a territorial government entity, but which is *empowered by the internal law of that State to exercise elements of governmental authority*, shall also be considered as an act of the State under international law, provided that organ was acting in that capacity in the case in question.' (4)

One might therefore consider whether Cidecorp or GTZ is performing any governmental function or acting with governmental authority in selling the anti-aircraft missile system. The rationale behind the above draft article is to prevent States from avoiding their international responsibilities by delegating those functions to other entities such as public limited companies. One would have to know the corporate functions and powers of GTZ and Cidecorp and the relevant municipal laws of States S and T to ascertain what they were entitled to do without government approval. It is possible that State S and/or State T were encouraging the export of arms systems.

An important factor in this area is the authority which the State may have exercised over the activities of either GTZ or Cidecorp. When one looks at the judgments of the *Nicaragua Case: Nicaragua* v *United States (Merits)* (5) – involving, inter alia, United States support for the Contra rebels – and the *Hostages Case: United States* v *Iran* (6) it is the degree of control which is crucial to attribute the action to the State. One has therefore to consider what is the State of nationality of Cidecorp and, having determined this, is either State S or State T responsible for its action in selling the missile system?

Having considered the issue of imputability it is also necessary to turn one's attention to the issue of State responsibility and the fault theory.

> 'It is often said that a State is not responsible to another State for unlawful acts committed by its agents unless such acts are committed wilfully and maliciously or with culpable negligence.' (7)

This is not, it must be said, universally agreed upon: the authorities are divided. Opposing the fault theory is the objective theory which argues that once an unlawful act has taken place and an injury has resulted and that act or omission was committed by an agent of the State (see above) then that State will be responsible to the injured State.

The leading case in this area, the *Corfu Channel Case (Merits): United Kingdom* v *Albania* (8), is advanced as supporting both theories. A British warship was damaged by a mine in the Corfu Channel, an international strait but also comprising Albanian territorial waters. The British government argued that Albania had laid the mines. The ICJ rejected this argument for lack of evidence but held Albania liable because it failed to act once it *knew* of the mines. Once Albania knew of the danger, it was obliged to warn other nations' shipping. The fact that Albania was held responsible for the activities in its waters would incline towards the objective theory but the mention of 'knowledge' would incline towards the subjective or fault theory.

In the present case it may be argued that once either State S or State T (see discussion above) allowed the respective companies to export arms to an insurgent group then that State should be held liable for the consequences. The international unlawful act is the selling of the arms to the Beta Liberation Movement (BLM) which is contrary to art 2(7) of the UN Charter as it is an interference in the domestic affairs of another State. It may also be a violation of art 2(4) as it involves the use of force (albeit indirectly) against the territorial integrity of another State. State S or State T should therefore be held responsible for the subsequent loss of life of the nationals of States U and V and the destruction of State U's aircraft.

The fault theory was discussed in the *Home Missionary Society Claim* (9) which considered the responsibility of the British government for the damage inflicted upon American property as a result of a civil disturbance in the British Protectorate of Sierra Leone. The United Kingdom was not held responsible for the damage as the civil disturbance was not foreseeable even though the catalyst was the imposition of an unpopular tax by the colonial authorities.

In the present case the BTM made no secret of its intention to use the missiles against State U's military aircraft. It could be argued that it was not foreseeable that they would be used against a reconnaissance aircraft. Whether or not this argument would succeed would depend upon whether the markings and shape of the aircraft were significantly different. It should also be pointed out that in the *Home Missionary Society Claim* (9) it was stressed that the United Kingdom had a sovereign right to levy taxes. It cannot be argued that a State has a sovereign right to provide missiles to insurgents in another State. The 'fault theory' might be on firmer ground in relation to the possible liability for the death of the military advisers from State V. It is possible to argue that it was not foreseeable that military advisers from another State would be present in State U's aircraft.

If State responsibility is established then the issue of remedies needs to be discussed. Damages may be claimed for the actual loss resulting from the damage or injury suffered. Thus, damages may be granted to State U for the loss of its aircraft and the death of its nationals. State V may also argue for damages in respect of the deaths of its military advisers. The damages may reflect the actual material damage (the loss of the aircraft) as well as damages for the loss of life of the aircrew and the military advisers. Damages may be awarded by an international tribunal to reflect the insult to the national honour of State U. An apology may also be demanded from the claimant State, as was given by Spain in the *Borchgrave Case: Belgium* v *Spain* (10).

To sum up, the claims that may arise from the events outlined will depend upon which State is the State of nationality of the company. If the actions of the company can be imputed to either State S or T then the issue of responsibility will have to be addressed. The problem does not indicate which possible tribunals might have jurisdiction, and if there are none then the issue may be dealt with by an ad hoc bi-lateral or tri-lateral agreement. The 'good offices' of, for example, the Secretary-General may be utilised, as was the case following the sinking of the *Rainbow Warrior* and the subsequent dispute between France and New Zealand.

References

(1) (1970) ICJ Rep p3
(2) *International Law* (3rd ed) p234
(3) (1928) PCIJ Rep Series A No 17 p29
(4) Quoted in *Starke's International Law* (11th ed 1994), p279 – the italics are those of *Starke's International Law*
(5) (1986) ICJ Rep p14
(6) (1980) ICJ Rep p3 (see also the Suggested Solution to Question 4(a))
(7) See *Starke's International Law* (11th ed 1994), p282, which refers to Judge Krylou's dissenting opinion in the *Corfu Channel (Merits) Case* (1949) ICJ Rep p4

References (continued)

(8) (1949) ICJ Rep p4
(9) (1920) 6 RIAA 42
(10) (1937) PCIJ Rep Series A/B No 72

QUESTION 9

'The 1994 Agreement relating to the "implementation" of the United Nations Convention on the Law of the Sea, 1982, represents a victory for states opposed to the principles originally embodied in Part XI of the Convention.'

Discuss.

SUGGESTED SOLUTION TO QUESTION 9

General Comment

This is a rather narrow question involving a detailed knowledge of Part XI of the Law of the Sea Convention 1982, which relates to the deep sea-bed. The candidate should be aware of the background to the original section of the convention dealing with the deep sea-bed and how the General Assembly Resolution in this matter influenced the original draft.

The reasons for the opposition to the original draft should be understood and how the opposition of the developed world influenced the 1994 Agreement.

Skeleton Solution

Nature and status of deep sea-bed.

GA Res 2749 and its influence on the Convention.

The terms of the 1982 Convention and the International Sea-Bed Authority.

The role of the 'Enterprise'; transfer of technology.

Opposition of developed world.

The terms of the 1994 Agreement.

Conclusion.

Suggested Solution

Part XI of the Convention is addressed to the 'Area' and it is this geographical entity, and its legal definition and the rights of exploitation which have been the source of controversy in the international community and which delayed the coming into force of the Law of the Sea Convention 1982. The 'Area' refers to the deep sea-bed and was the subject of disagreement in international law as to its status. The two opposing theories were that, on the one hand, the sea-bed was res nullius and therefore capable of occupation and appropriation and, on the other hand, that the sea-bed shared the same characteristics as the high seas and could not be appropriated by either States or other legal entities. The reason for this subject matter taking on a controversial character was the possibility of exploiting the deep sea-bed and the minerals therein. The General Assembly saw fit to pass a resolution on the matter before even a definition of the area in question was reached. General Assembly Res 2749 (1970) refers to an area of the sea-bed and the ocean floor beyond the limits of national jurisdiction *the precise limits of which are yet to be defined.*

The controversy did not, however, centre so much on the definition of the area as on who was to receive the fruits of the exploitation. The resolutions in art 1 to the resources of the sea-bed, beyond the national jurisdiction, as being the common heritage of mankind. Article 7 speaks of the exploration of the area and its resources being carried out for the benefit of mankind as a whole. The precise legal status of this resolution is unclear and although the resolution did not attract any votes against it, nevertheless it was not authoritatively argued that the resolution represented customary international law (1).

The Resolution nevertheless acted as a spur to the matter being placed on the agenda at United Nations Convention on the Law of the Sea 1982 (UNCLOS III). Article 9 of the Resolution called for an international regime to apply to the area and the setting-up of international machinery 'to give effect to its provisions ... established by an international treaty'.

The Law of the Sea Convention attempted to establish such an international regime. The deep sea-bed was firstly defined (the 'Area') as the sea-bed, ocean floor and subsoil beyond the limits of national jurisdiction: art 1 Law of the Sea Convention. The Convention then went to state that the 'Area and its resources are the common heritage of mankind': art 136. An International Sea-bed authority was proposed as the organisation through which activities in the Area were to be controlled and organised. Membership of the Authority was to include all States parties to the Convention: art 156. The Convention then went on to propose that the financial and other economic benefits derived from activity in the Area should be applied by the Authority for the benefit of mankind as a whole, irrespective of the geographical location of States, whether coastal or land locked, taking into particular consideration the interests and needs of developing States: art 149.

The above presented issues of conflict between the developed world and the developing world. Because they had the economic capability, the developed States wished exploitation in the Area to be conducted by their own national enterprises, while the developing States argued for the establishment of an international body to regulate exploitation of the Area's resources. The Convention put forward a Solomonic compromise. The

International Sea-Bed Authority delegated the activity of exploitation of the sea-bed to one of its institutions, the 'Enterprise', with the other half going to a commercial enterprise; this was known as the parallel access basis. The Convention also stated in art 44 that there should be a transfer of technology relating to activities in the Area, from the developed countries and their mining companies to the Authority and the developing States. Articles 150 and 151 sought to regulate the development of the Area with the object of controlling and stabilising mineral prices and thereby protecting those developing countries and their economies which are dependent on the export of raw materials.

The above proposals were unacceptable to the developed world. The developed world argued that the effect would be harmful to their economic well-being as their companies were the most advanced technologically and the most able to exploit and benefit from the exploitation of the sea-bed. It was an undertaking involving a considerable expenditure of capital, and the proposed regulation of prices went against their free-market principles. On 29 January 1982 President Reagan put forward a number of amendments necessary to effect a United States ratification of the treaty. He argued against restriction of deep sea mining in order to control prices and demand. The United States also stated its opposition to the mandatory transfer of technology. The viewpoint of the United States was also shared by other western States such as Germany and the United Kingdom, which together with the United States refused to sign the treaty while, for instance, France, Russia and Japan refused to ratify the agreement. Moreover the developed world enacted legislation enabling its companies to engage in exploration and exploitation of the deep sea-bed. Further, the developed world in some instances reached arrangements with each other so as to prevent them granting overlapping national licences (2).

This refusal of the developed world, with the exception of Iceland, resulted in an impasse.

The opposition of Part XI of the Law of the Sea Convention led to a rethinking of the concepts and ideas behind Part XI. This was put forward by a UN General Assembly Resolution in 1994 (GA Res 48/263). The Resolution addressed itself to the implementation of Part XI. The Resolution urged the States to adopt a revised version of Part XI. The effect of this 'Implementing Agreement' is to accommodate the views of the developed world. The assertion that the deep sea-bed is the common heritage of mankind is still present but the workings of the Agreement reflect the demand for a market-oriented system. The role of the Enterprise which was to carry out exploration on a parallel access basis (half the sea-bed to be exploited by commercial enterprises and the other half by the Enterprise) has been diminished. The Enterprise was originally placed in an advantageous position in that the commercial operation was saddled with the initial exploration costs. Under the terms of the Implementation Agreement this obligation is no longer present. Moreover the transfer of technology is no longer a bureaucratic directive, rather it is governed by market principles.

The effect of the above was to allay the fears of the developed world and it led to the ratification of the Law of the Sea Convention by, for example, the United States in July 1994, and the treaty came into force in November 1994. The 1994 Agreement is an effective 'rewrite' of the original. The 'dirigiste' character of the original has been changed. The dropping of a mandatory transfer of technology and of arbitrary limits on production reflects not only the importance and influence of the developed world in this area but also the acceptance of a market-oriented system since the original was drafted.

References

(1) See the Suggested Solution to Question 1 for a discussion of this issue

(2) *Starke's International Law* (11th ed), p254